P9-EDR-390

In Favor of Lightning

Wesleyan New Poets

In Favor of Lightning

Barbara Molloy-Olund

Wesleyan University Press
Middletown, Connecticut

Some of the poems in this book appeared originally in *The Black Warrior Review, Chiaroscuro, Field, Fine Madness, Poetry Northwest,* and *Sonora Review.* The lines from ''Prelude'' are reprinted from *Translations from the Poetry of Rainer Maria Rilke* by M. D. Herter Norton by permission of W. W. Norton & Company, Inc. Copyright 1938 by W. W. Norton & Company, Inc. Copyright renewed 1966 by M. D. Herter Norton.

All inquiries and permissions requests should be addressed to the Publisher, Wesleyan University Press, 110 Mt. Vernon Street, Middletown, Connecticut 06457.

Distributed by Harper & Row Publishers, Keystone Industrial Park, Scranton, Pennsylvania 18512.

Library of Congress Cataloging-in-Publication Data
Molloy-Olund, Barbara, 1958–
  In favor of lightning.
  (Wesleyan new poets)
  I. Title.   II. Series.
PS3563.041915   1987   811'.54   86-32441
ISBN 0-8195-2132-9 (alk. paper)
ISBN 0-8195-1133-1 (pbk.   :   alk. paper)

Manufactured in the United States of America

First Edition

Wesleyan New Poets

To my Mother and Father
and for Jeffrey

you lift quite slowly a black tree
and place it against the sky: slender, alone.
And you have made the world . . .

Rainer Maria Rilke

Contents

1. In Retrospect, the Sky

In Retrospect, the Sky

Heaven was always a little to the north
of our lives, an invisible star
in transit above
our dinner table.

And if, for years at a time
there was silence at that end,
it was only because God
was a distracted man, probably
poring over his work
much like my own father.

It was important to remember
that though we were alone
in our sorrow, pain, like a shadow,
did nothing to distinguish us.
My knees touched my sister's
and I prayed for the safe return of a plane
carrying my mother, I prayed
for an athlete's body, and then
I prayed to stop sinning.

It had everything to do with timing.
Still, each night I slept
to one side of the bed
making room for the angel
of the lord, imagining our encounter
and knowing it would be nothing
like I imagined, but more
like the first crude kiss
in summer, my back pressed
against a road sign.

Much later it happened.
I lay on my back in a field.
The tiny, light blue stars were there
hovering in clusters like mosquitos
and the angel's face was tan and warm.
He had a mustache and he drifted
quietly over me, then hurried away
leaving nothing, not even a secret
path, only the green weeds
that whispered and went on.

In a car years later,
my mother turned and said,
there must not be a God.
Or he was deaf or callous.
She wasn't serious
but her clear voice and the way
she talked out the window—
I thought she could see something
out there, something beneath
the neat, dry rows of corn.

The Proximity of Sparrows

So I began to listen to them,
the sparrows,
their wings in a panic as they hovered
at our second-story window,
to see vanity as they dove
and then rose again

at the ledge where dry bread crumbs
had them skimming close.
I remembered one zoo's famous walrus
in his marine tank, who would nose up
to the green glass and knock gently

as if to be let in on
the secret that stared back at him.

For years I thought the eyes in museum paintings
could sense my meditation.
So it was always difficult to stare

for any length of time at a reclining nude
without feeling an embarrassing kinship.
I felt to view that ancient moment
was to fall inside it. History
is not unlike this:

a window, a bird. Eventually
I'm looking in on
my own primitive likeness.

Cemetery near Gaslight Village

Meanwhile, it is rumored
that the real angel
is one he came to each night
with flowers
as though he could win her back
with flowers.

Sister David Will Not Ride
in an Automobile

Then, the answer must have been small
to be folded inside her habit.
On the blackboard it was the blank space
in an equation
where a number would soon line up
with dignity.

Her manly shoes, her oval face.
She walks a stone path to the convent.
A veil, an umbrella: such order
cannot love us.

Sister David will not ride
in an automobile.
She will be the black butterfly
in the courtyard.
When I am sick
she will lead me to the tabernacle
where the green air will always be sour.

My soul at this age
is compared to a classroom window—
transparent and on a slant.
To correct this
she wears black.
My nakedness, she says, is a temple.

One day I dream they have to pry me out of it.

Years Later

Years later, pain
slips over the roof
like a constellation, beyond
these disciplined trees, the car
easing into the drive
or the house I drift through,
straightening things.

I stand beside the heroic
furniture, battered bicycles,
a lawn as solemn as my face
to keep up. I aim my cigarette
skyward.

None of it is mine. True,
I've named my children.
The calls I place to them
in the middle of the night
reach further than forgiveness.

One by one I check their rooms
for windows left open on rain.
Light sleeps on the beds
and I recall the dream I am afraid
to finish
of things as they are:

the furnace moaning into the hallway's
long hush, a wish for birth.
And when wind rubs the door
I believe it is the daughter
who came in late one night
with breasts.

Along the Mississippi

And I believe I saw reality, floating;
a houseboat coasting across a river
dragging its bouquet of shade
and looking like a traveling church
had slid away from its southern setting

for a life of pleasure. On deck, four or five
couples sipped cocktails in the moonlight.
Atmosphere was paper lights, orange and red,
such brash colors
on the soft reputation of water.
But these nine or ten were not on earth,
not really. They were singing

a song which dated them
as they strolled in their t-shirts.
Their voices hung in the air afterward,
embarrassing the dark
by being darker. I remember best

the woman who stumbled
on the wet terrace. That night
she was no one's child, nobody's mother. She was drunk

and she leaned hard against her partner.
It was one of a series of summer nights
in which the stars had been dead
for a long time. I remember

she was clumsy. She let the glass slip
from her hand, the pieces shatter
at her bare feet. On another night
the man she held might not have laughed so quickly
but he knew they were floating.

There was a current, the heart
of the water was everywhere.

Poem

I bring a damp rag into the room
where you lie in the shyness
of ordinary fever. In your dream
the door clicks and you moan once,
as if words had been buried alive
and only the vowel can lift out now, unsophisticated
and lonely as light
cultivating a downward crack in the window.

Here, on earth, we have been permitted to come so close.
A pine's blue hair brushes the roof.
Einstein talked to the Universe from a bare room
with one, lousy pencil.

Maybe a woman takes her teeth out at night,
lays them aside in a glass on the table.
Her teeth from her mouth on a table
at night. An agreement is that deep.

2. Here on Earth

Rainfall in the Midwest

A fine rain comes down
to the street. The shadow of the fine rain
is the whole sky
divided by a door. And what you hear
is loosely like the flapping of hundreds
of souls, if they are, flying
just now over the wheat.

The bum tack slides from the wall
in the damp air, several invisible years
rub together a blue light of wires.
The clouds are dark, the yellow pears
twice-bright in the grass.
The street flashes

and the sound in the leaves stretches
like that superstition: lightning
will not strike the side of a barn
where swallows are nesting, where it is night
slowly and with a smell, a deep smell
of the living.

In Favor of Lightning

Nothing I've seen is like this
lightning as it drops to its hands
over a quiet barn
releasing its brief self in spasms.

Behind it, nothing. A cool night,
an occasional house drifts past. Tomorrow,
that house, this air, these weeds
will not appear stricken.
But, I don't want to think

about tomorrow.
I would rather watch these trees
flash and spring forward
with the kind of fleeting, impetuous nerve
we manage only once or twice
our whole lives.

There is no one for miles.
There never was, and north and south
are interrupted by that long strand of light
overtaking the sky by shivering
through itself. There is fear that, like rain,
sounds human

but has no **voice**. Not mine or yours
and not the **voice** of someone
who loves **us**. **Fear** like a white streak
coming from **behind** to enter the mirror
or those dashes in the road
which erase **longevity**.

How transparent lightning makes everything!
The rigid **fence**, the blind moths
that crash **like** seconds
against the **windshield**.
I can see **myself**

there, where **lightning**
dies of **brilliance**
over a sudden pond.

Heirloom

That evening, the blackbird dropped
to our roof again. Packaged in its small bones
was the same moment
and a cool song that turned, "what if,
what if, what if," until I had to look up again
to see how it perched, slick in its folds,   ·
delicate breast tilted like the afternoon's ornament.

Again I thought how it would fit in my palm
and feel as good there as money.
I could imagine it, stealing up to the roof ledge,
being that close, which was terrifying.
I love you, someone says into space
and everything outside that voice is changed—

I think this is the story. The blackbird
came here, absorbed in its birdhood,
and the stars came, one by one, sealed
in their beauty. And it wasn't enough
to be haunted by them, either. Or to haunt.
It was cruel. Time inside flowers and all that.

Black bird, violet sky, if God put perfection
inside you, who put our bones inside jealousy?

Such confusion, as if I'd lost you
and now you'll cause nothing but grief.

Today, the relatives aren't speaking.
You are the reason, the first heirloom, a death
to be gathered around and divided between us.

But wasn't this always the story
long before you came here,
about how love was given over,
handed down in unequal shares?

Money

Our last couple of dollars
are maple leaves
curled at the bottom of a yellow jar.
What good is it?
Tonight the pipes will ache
like an elbow left out in the snow
and you will sleep
with your teeth clenched
remembering a bottle of vintage wine
we drank without occasion.

Our last couple of dollars are cinders,
and on the slope a dark horse
is a poor thing. By the quiet road,
mailboxes extend their open hands.
Why does the front-room window stare
at a vanishing phone line
as though the world were truly round?

The world was never round.
It is the poor room my mother mentioned
where light is stern and far off
and the gentlest face is suspicious.
A dream smells of forgotten milk.
If you open the closets—musty air.
There is dust on a mirror,

our hands, everything
that surprises us because it is here:
eyeglasses, lampshades, moonlight
on the curious furniture
no one can pay for.

Knot

Like someone who tries to piece
odd dreams together,
I walk through the house collecting
strands of hair from the drain, the towels, the table,
forgetting that it belongs to a time
I barely acknowledge

and have no memory of:
when I might have been an animal
and further back
to when the animal might have been fruit.
Tonight I slit a pomegranate open
and learned from the bright seed cluster
that fruit was once star. And what was star anyway
but something dense, something old,
the inside of a word. Here is my breath,

this dry stuff rain left on our kitchen window,
my breath which will be visible in winter.
Here against the white sink
or floating on the water's skin
is my old hair, the fur I shed. In my palm
still soft as though alive, it is a rust-colored clump.
I could almost hand it back to my grandmother

for its texture, the way it still attempts to curl:
dark cobweb, braid, strand, feather.
At night she puts her hand inside
its warmth. When she loosens the braid
I see the tree. When she combs through it
I expect she'll pick up stars, leaves, cinders,
a knot more dense than words.
She said, *I'll die when I'm ready.*
And then it was over.
And then it was winter.

Take the Swallows with You

Take the swallows with you.
Those almost mechanical birds
came too close in their tentative sweeping.
Now I see how the gloves of their wings
are tapered, so that even as they lift away
a whole school seems to point back
as if to remind me of how we stood
arm in arm near a public building.
This is too much like a dream
where walking away becomes a complicated step.
Take the swallows with you
and their shadows, five papercuts on the grass.

Take the shadow of the flowers with you.
I am afraid I will injure them.
The ghost of deep attachment
is in their faces. Even the ones near the river
are ankle deep in sentiment.
To look at them is to feel sorry
for the way a thing blossoms overnight.
Take the flowers with you.
Their shadows are glass.

Take the window with you.
If only you tug it will all come down
piece by piece in the way one thing leads
to another. Notice how cold it gets
as if leaves are blowing in
and rain falls on your easy sleep.
Think how silly a man and woman are
without a window. No moon nearby
and the room suddenly empty
without its view of water.

Blockstarken

On a visit to Germany, a woman read the word "Blockstarken" in the
print of an old poster. She later learned there is no such word in the
German language.

They must have taken our breath with them,
these words, now no more than the substance of feathers,
husks of decrepit objects, dust you find in the crack of a leaf.
Some, longer than was necessary, over the earth with their shadows,
curved precisely and were never seen again.

I suppose this is why we sometimes stop, look at the ground
while talking, and why we'll need to talk louder as we go on,
why the trees appear to hang there inhaling it all:
what we are saying, what we are not saying as the blocks darken.
Inside the snowflake right now

languishing, wet, falling slowly, must be bits of old, lost conversation:
two people on stools near the window, their lips moving,
hands folded humbly under the table,
or their hands moving like white fires. And probably
what they are saying is what they will be saying

as the breath goes out of them, before they've agreed on anything,
before the soup comes. Who can say? Maybe we are surrounded
by a music that remembers us. I don't know.
I'm washing glasses and I get this word stuck inside my head
that was buried in Germany like the jaw of the last man

to say it, and now he could very well be singing
through the hollow wine glass as I let my finger slide
cryptically around the rim. Blocks darken. Blocks darken
but only in my own language. The single word for snow
collects in the black notch of the single word for tree

and out in the white shade a weathervane's tin scales
start moving. Now a small gust is talking. Now something other
than the rust it has become holds it together, keeps it up
like a solitary partner waltzing. Tipping each wine glass
upside down, I think, this could be my mother inside me

or just boredom
but I find myself singing this word
immersed in its delicate nonsense. I find myself
lining the glasses up while singing
as if to keep my place in the universe in place.

Beginnings

A cloud might have moved into their bodies
for them to sleep like that, snouts grinding
into mud, each pig a raw silhouette
finding such exotic contortions that you think
of kneeling to rearrange their discomfort.

You think to them you must seem a distant industry.
Their eyes barely hold your shape
and you're vague as the rib shed by Adam.
You are the upright shadow whose feet
flatten the earth like fruit dropping.

Slowly the farm takes in the story of creation,
each acre exposed, grey as a dream of self-sufficiency.
Here are the spiritual slop, the buckets, the moon
and the animals' unconscious bleatings. Here,
the carnal state before it weakened,

and here you are touching your face,
knowing it as a strange appendage, leaning
it over the pen like a flower that grows
between the difficult border
of starlight and slaughter.

3. How It Begins

October, a Parade

Do they wave and hear the music
because the flowers are just now shivering
or do the flowers shiver because of them,
because, like weather, they are just passing?
I don't think it matters. Only
that it is October now. Each oblong garden
is a flag and for each flag, a murder,
and last night I dreamed a flower
so red it was black, and then grey
and then it was gone. This evening our fathers
have come out of the woodwork
to stand at the curb under the seamless sky.
And when the whole thing is over
they will look like the sky. Gigantic. Modest.

I think this is what the sound of horns
is trying to get at
as the people flow out of their houses to watch,
exhausted by a madness that carries them home.
It is October. Leaves slip slowly off
the elms, not unlike the anonymous dead
who are in no hurry, who have fallen behind.
And as if to remind ourselves of the nature of horror,
the sky breaks into blossom, into a fire that glitters

white as skeletal snow. Pieces of it whistle down
and the strange smoke lingers. October,
the month might also be self-conscious
with wasp husks on the stairs,
with trees remembering how to die—
a beauty that hesitates, a sound of bullets
that might otherwise embarrass the planet
blowing over.

Waking When It's Still Dark

Part of the moon is still there, like glass
on a filthy corner of Gilbert Street. The part
of the moon still there could be the commotion
I woke to, a moon so bright I can almost hear it
humming. I got up unable to solve
whatever it was in my sleep. Now with pins falling
out of my hair, I prepare these rooms for walking.
My bare feet break into the stiff floor. My white
face haunts the three streaked windows. Yesterday,
as she explained depression to me, a friend said,
"Unlike anxiety, it is distinguished by too much
sleeping." How much is too much, I wondered,
thinking there might be some fine line showing
where my dream had stopped and how
I had only been lying in its residue, a flabby
place where I rested breathing deeply of my own excess.
A sleep like waking in so many ways except I could
only lie there, when I might have been reading
or sewing on a button.
Later, I looked up the word "anxiety"
in the dictionary. And, as usual, another word
caught my attention: Anting—
the deliberate placing by some passerine birds
of living ants among the feathers. Remarkable,
but the description was so plain, the words themselves
so deliberate they all but missed the inspired
facts: living ants among the feathers . . .

ants living among feathers! Tiny black ants
tucked into birds. The cardinal flying around the shed
might be wearing them. Ants like a faint field
of static. Meanwhile my eyes, like the slippery pages
of the book, pick up nothing. Not how many,
not even what for, and certainly not how it would feel.
So that I have to imagine it like needles
in my own left hand when it is a dumb extremity
falling asleep and I rub and rub
to bring the world back into me, the rush of it
into my wrist and down into each finger.

I think I've known of these ants,
accumulated by birds until they are integral
to the bird's machinery. As a child
I thought insects were marching
under the bark of the tree to put the tree
together branch by branch. I never asked why,
trusting the earth to have its earthly reasons,
sleeping with a greenish rock under my pillow.
Now I confide in the dictionary
which is like the light in this room
for all it accumulates in passing.
It tells me anxiety is a perturbation
whose cause is no longer available. Anxiety
like the moon, I suppose. Depression
the way a green stone loses its feeling
in my grip.

Red House, Red Leaves

She said she dreamt of garbage blowing.
A day that was raining leaves. Autumn. Trees
at the peak of some color—gold, plum,

sober. She was making an effort to feel better,
saying it like the time of year could hear her,
had been there itself, and reached with its barest

look across the room, cutting like sun into the grains of wood,
the part in her hair. There was only enough sorrow for now,
where, before it was bigger, longer,

more abstract, a sort of floating terror.
I walked around and around in the alley that night
with the noise of the leaves like props from her dream,

and the smell of their rotting, like the air
was escorting them sincerely back to their salt.

Report

Last night I dreamed a woman in dirty clothes
and holding a baby turned up at the home
of a jazz pianist. I don't know whether he was great
but he was almost blind, as some are.
Don't ask me how they got there,

the mother, and her baby all covered
in stale blankets. The dream
didn't ask. I don't know whether later,
say, a year from now,
they're all living happily

with the man playing piano in the background
while the clean baby screams, as they do:
a flower in a Dixie Cup in the window
and the mother wearing shoes again, the weeds
in the garden turning into snapdragons
and the neighbors wondering "What's he up to?"
as they do.

I don't even know if the mother got there
in a beat-up Lincoln, or if she had to hitchhike
with the kid sleeping between her knees
in a strange automobile, but a baby sleeps anywhere,
a baby sleeps like a bale of hay through a storm.

I don't know if the mother had been walking all day
on a hot street in Florida with the baby hurting her arm
like her own muscle. I only know they were there
and this guy was a jazz pianist, probably retired.

These details were as clear as a minute in the dark
finding its way into your gut.
All three were there, huddled together

as if inside a tornado that would lift up lives
and set them down again, coolly.
Such dreams are not messy like storms though,
and mine didn't say whether the pianist would die

one day in his sleep, senile, falling in his own house,
indiscriminately. I remember the three of them were stuck
that way: mother, baby, pianist. My dream wanted them
there, at that moment when they were alive
before the next moment. I'm telling you

because I thought you might want to know.

We worry so much about things . . .
mothers, babies with soft skulls, trees crashing
onto the roof for no reason, old people
hearing music all of a sudden, and from nowhere.

My Friend's Father

We found *Playboys* in his narrow bedroom closet.
My friend got up on the bed and pulled them down.

I had to let her turn the pages. It was her house.
I remember she seemed to be taking a long time. I was eleven.
Maybe everything seemed to take a long time.

I might have touched my breasts once, twice, in the shower.
Probably I hardly touched them. I would let the bathroom fog up
so the other rooms, with my family in them, disappeared

and the field with its monotonous chiccer of insects
went blank on the other side of the window.
I might have known then

that there were women, somewhere, who would do this,
what the blond woman on the dimpled pages was doing:
holding her own up in her own hands, hefting them up, both

of them, enormous, and creamy, and the real thing.
Despite their proportions, you could see how they belonged to her,
to the swell of her pale hairdo and her waxy fingernails

resting, almost eclipsed, under their weight.
What got me at the time was not only the woman's fullness
or the way she looked down at herself, down at them,

like she had a right to look down at them—
what got me was that she did this on a glass boat,
a boat surrounding her nakedness on all sides

by the push of blue water. I stared
and my friend lingered on this page for a minute,
and I couldn't place either the woman or the water,

but there they were, nothing between them but the ingenious
windows. In one picture, she leaned with her right breast
nearly smashed against the clear, rushing walls.

"Big ones," my friend said out loud. "What big ones," she'd say,
or simply in her throat she'd whisper, "Big ones."
Like they were an aberration, but worse,

like she hadn't even noticed the boat, like the boat had gone
completely under and over her, the way the plump woman
might slip completely beyond her father's bedroom,

basking and sprawling and spread over two pages.
And for whom? The two of us, my friend who was younger
and still slept under a frilly canopy, and me,

thinking her father would come in at any minute
and find us there in his room, lying on his unmade bed
whose sheets smelled of lozenges and some kind of soap

that smelled like a father. Her father,
whose one hobby was fixing bicycles. There were bicycle
parts on the dining-room table, black heart-shaped seats,

junked handlebars. Always their house was like that—
a mess. What on earth was the woman on the glass deck doing
when he would be home any minute, grumpy

and with a long stripe of sweat under each arm, her father
who would never in his life climb onto a glass boat
and ride around the sea with a nude woman?

On the Porch in the Evening

You can't pet them. These are the ones
the fields kept—burrs, infestations, sores
near their eyes. They'll work their teeth
over birds they've crippled, snatch what moves
in the air. The tiniest death inspires them.

Why do you listen? Tonight they only hurt
one another, carrying the hatred of their own
species clear as the marble of each eye. But,
they're not committed: they go at it
like schoolchildren. You listen.

Braced beneath the exposed wire, you try
to separate the slope of dark from the lawn's edge,
their weight from stumps or far muscular outlines.
Only a true extrovert could conceive of this,
of them, the way a boy might load one up with a firecracker

then stand back as it grows inflated, arched
to where it will burst and scatter its teased fur.
They look like that now, spraying first, knowing
only that they will mate or fight, sometimes
in the crawl space, sometimes the ghosted garden

and never pretty. The one is crouched rigid as a saint
and the other is clumsy for all its machinery.
Often one will dig in the middle of it, a sane act,
a private act, a need you can almost understand
as you'd hear speech in their plaintive sulking,

or think in your dreams how a reptile is folding.
When it's over they slant away—distracted tails
your only marker for having seen them. Why
do you do it? You go down with a pan of warm milk,
place it on that spot of grass where the ground is cold

and think how it must have hurt, how at least
they'd be hungry. If you stand under the moon
like the curator of something—what is it?

How It Begins

Someone yells "fuck you,"
from a car window.
The car peels down the road,
its motor dragging behind.
Maybe this is how each month should
begin, with a conclusive "fuck you"
from an open window. It occurs to me
to put down the can of tuna
and to pick up the distance
between myself and that kid
whose face is pressed against the wind,
whose hair flies like sparks
from his flung cigarette.
Sometimes it's the radio that's obscene.
Two kids are sunbathing on a rooftop.
You can't blame them for how
their glowing bodies deflect, or for
their songs pumped into the sky in the background:
everything metallic down to their skin
and the waves the heat makes
and the waves from the music's far pulse
and the grass as content as light inside
a grape. It may as well belong too.
And that cloud, a blast of color at its rim.

Give them the cloud. Give them the whole month
of March if they want it. It's only
the distance between myself and *fuck you*
to a time when my mother used to say, "Music?
It sounds like a sick dog whimpering,"
when I knew it was the sound of
love driving through its prime
and you had to be there to appreciate it—
right inside the car, your hair on fire at its edge,
keeping time for everyone else who was tired of it.
Otherwise you had to be the one watching
them cruise your neighborhood, knowing
they were headed for a beach, seeing their car
burst into flames at the edge of your town,
without you. Without
you.

Imperfect Elegy

Dying changes everything. Your face
in candlelight, the light itself defining

the tilt of your chin.
Your hair is nearly gold now, your grief

nearly perfect as that time of day
when it settles over your features.

You will not be beautiful again,
but comfortable

as you sit on the other side of the table
and say, head drooping,

"I am so lonely," to your food.
Like the government or the waitress, I offer you

the discreet white napkin dipped in water.
I push the bread toward you. "That's better," I say.

But it's food that softens you now, rolls
trickling butter, chicken which you tear into.

You are separating the crisp skin from the meat as always,
saying you'll be fat when they find you

and you don't give a damn who hears—
meaning you will order another drink, that you're about to cry,

and I am not in it. I am like the people in the painting
of the winter night above your head, or the others

at the doorway standing flushed and lively in the draft.
Their happiness is the barest evidence of your dying,

here in the restaurant as I look at you.

And don't I know, you ask, what separates the rich
from the poor?

"This." You point to your temple. The sudden
clairvoyant in you is pure. Your eyes flash green,

and your hand upsets the brandy. How could I?
I see the dull paneling in the background

and the carnation at each table
so unimpressed with us, as I wipe the drippings

from your chin, as if to prepare you for some picture.
And I am not in it,

though I love you with a mind to carry you
like a mirror out of here, or like the poor

for whom the rules, whatever they are, are made.

Force

Even as we speak tonight, a tiny spider
is taking a June bug live. The web's stringy ingredient
is like a worn picture of itself death has taped
to a side beam. It breathes like leaves

undersea while we light a match or snap a beer open,
talking into a night as rich in its manure as its stars.
Or we are quiet, and we hear the quiet like a train
full of fruit passing. No one seems to know

where our first orders come from. But in theory
we must hear our fathers in the drunk man next door
tossing a melon rind to the driveway and shouting
at the boy, "I thought I told you to pick up the garbage."

There is no struggle but a tedium in the father's long shadow
and the boy crouching there. No theory but one that stretches
to include the boy who takes the dirty, fly-stung rind
in his hand, holding it away from his body like a lantern,

at that distance, anything, even a father's voice is soft.
In our chairs, on the porch, I suppose we have to twist
this boy's reason to please into love. We have to walk with him

back to the trash can and let our eyes sink
down the barrel where a wet, bright melon lies.
And when we come up again, the father is a shadow in the window

of the messy house that insults him. Just as if it was a project
passed down from one insect to another, a design
to be completed in a later life by its meaning,
the June bug throws itself right into

the web and hangs there, a withered hand in a threadbare pocket
and our talk goes around it. Our talk goes almost over our heads.
Someone walks indoors to change the record.
Someone opens another beer. No theory suggests

the light of a star recapitulates the first ugly and insulated
orders out of a loneliness of darkness for light
but then, someone says, "How clear it is tonight"
and we all look and we agree.

Who wouldn't want to be the first to say, "Let there
be light." Who wouldn't want to carry the boy
safely out of this life, saying, "There, there, it is over."
Even knowing it isn't. Even knowing it goes on with the web

expanding and contracting, the legs of the June bug twitching
as they cling. Who can't see himself there, swaying,
being rocked to sleep by his father, who says, "There now,
I didn't mean it, there."

Passenger

The fruit of my window
is the blackest segment.
I can brush my finger along the glass
and watch how the mark shrinks slowly
into opacity, like the thread of something live
across a river. A moment ago

there was a river when I looked down,
land angled and squared, but like the brain
studying the brain, above the clouds
we lose the reason for color. Up here
air resembles water.

When I used to clean the room we'd sleep in
of any trace of myself, shoving underthings
in a closet, hiding earrings, ashtrays,
even the book I'd been reading,
I was thinking you'd turn the light on
and find this life as it was, heaped on a chair.

Now it's not so much a question
of how to leave well enough alone
but how to leave at all.

About the Author

Barbara Molloy-Olund was born in Hinsdale, Illinois. She began writing poetry while studying at Southern Illinois University and she earned an M.F.A. at the University of Iowa Writers Workshop in 1985. She lives in Boston, where she teaches English and creative writing.

About the Book

In Favor of Lightning was composed in Meridien type by Monotype Composition Company of Baltimore, Maryland, printed on 60-pound Miami Book paper by Kingsport Press of Kingsport, Tennessee, and bound by Kingsport Press. The design was by Joyce Kachergis Book Design & Production of Bynum, North Carolina.

Wesleyan University Press, 1987